About the Author

Carl Patterson is originally from Jersey City, NJ. He is a licensed professional counselor and spoken-word performer. He has a bachelor's degree in psychology from the University of Central Oklahoma and a master's degree from Southern Nazarene University. In 2017 and 2023, Carl presented at Tedx. He's passionate about mental health and uplifting Black culture.

The Mis-Execution of a Black Son

Carl Patterson

The Mis-Execution of a Black Son

Olympia Publishers
London

www.olympiapublishers.com
OLYMPIA PAPERBACK EDITION

Copyright © Carl Patterson 2024

The right of Carl Patterson to be identified as author of
this work has been asserted in accordance with sections 77 and 78 of
the Copyright, Designs and Patents Act 1988.

All Rights Reserved

No reproduction, copy or transmission of this publication
may be made without written permission.
No paragraph of this publication may be reproduced,
copied or transmitted save with the written permission of the publisher,
or in accordance with the provisions
of the Copyright Act 1956 (as amended).

Any person who commits any unauthorised act in relation to
this publication may be liable to criminal
prosecution and civil claims for damage.

A CIP catalogue record for this title is
available from the British Library.

ISBN: 978-1-80439-620-9

This is a work of creative nonfiction. The events are portrayed to the best of the author's memory. While all the stories in this book are true, some names and identifying details have been changed to protect the privacy of the people involved.

First Published in 2024

Olympia Publishers
Tallis House
2 Tallis Street
London
EC4Y 0AB

Printed in Great Britain

Dedication

To my mom, Pattie.

Acknowledgments

Thank you to the many who have been a part of my story. All of you are acknowledged in my journey.

It took me a lifetime to write this book.

We have so far to go, yet we have come so far.

The Mis-Execution of a Black Son is inspired by the life-changing and triggering screams of George Floyd calling out to his late mother Larcenia Floyd as he was being suffocated by officer Derek Chauvin for almost nine minutes. I watched as the world watched on May 25, 2020; another Black man lost his life to police brutality. The eight-minute and forty-six-second video brought attention globally to the treatment of Black people at the hands of the police and ignited historic protests on essential topics such as race and policing.

    I remember my body being triggered and having a physical reaction to watching a Black man gasp for air until it was too late. I experienced every primary feeling you could imagine on an emotional wheel. I went from sadness to anger to fear to disgust. My body reacted to this tragic event by triggering my own trauma; leaving me drained, confused, and mostly hurt. When my body settled and my thoughts cleared, *The Mis-Execution of a Black Son* was born.

    During that emotional time, I asked myself these questions: Do they really know what it is like to be Black in America? Do they know the generational trauma existing within us as we try to function in spaces that seem less and less safe each and every day? Being without my own child, I quickly turned to the question of how tough it must be to raise a Black son in America. I wondered how Black mothers felt about raising young Black boys to men knowing their life was in danger every day. I wondered how my mother felt about raising me as a Black son in America.

    I set out to write emotional poems that provided a broad

view of the plight, pain, and resolve of Black men to overcome. *The Mis-Execution of a Black Son* is about educating, connecting, and healing. The poems on the surface express weaknesses disguised as unwavering strengths. I focused on themes of slavery, trauma, death, grief, brutality, hope, healing, vulnerability, resilience, and love. The poems are primarily written from the Black male perspective but the hope is to develop compassion within us all and to gain a better understanding of the work needed to relieve those of their internal and external suffering.

With these poems, I want to change the narrative for the many Black bodies unnecessarily harmed. I wanted to give a voice to those who have yet to use their voice or those who are in search for words to describe how they feel each day. These poems are presented in a raw and direct fashion to bring to light the reality of Black males searching for the safest path to freedom from their traumas and the pain caused by a society making it incredibly tough for them to exist in peace.

My execution and the execution of other Black boys and men have been falsely advertised. As I wrote each poem, sharing personal struggles and tragedies, I was constantly reminded that *I'm not dead yet!*

I

us

when asked about my hometown i give the address of the atlantic. go see the bones of the Black bodies and let their femurs be your atlas. go see the frigidness in which we exist. go see the trail of kin. but don't worry. the water bites but it doesn't break skin. you may recoil from the predictable sting. the first wave may swallow and submerge you but don't worry, you were raised to resurface. the cold current runs down the crown. streaks past your eyebrows. and restores you like nothing else can. you will drift free. the water rapidly rushing over your skin. deep sea dweller. you will embrace the surface while the depths remain civilization for my kin. far from us. they profess the present as the pre-set. but we still live at sea. trace my lineage back to the pregnant African women. captured by captors who considered them sick and disruptive. condemning them with calculated excitement. so they were thrown off slave ships to drown. cast to sea. but don't worry. the water bites but it doesn't break skin. a captive starves so sharks can swim. common is the trauma of alternate narratives. every word you cannot say. everything we don't talk about. suspends wholeness, reunion, return. we learn to grieve people we never met. and own pain we never lived. our mothers nurture Black boys they never birthed. holding Black girls close to their bosom to keep them warm. that foul odor that hovers resting in the breeze. the smell when something you thought was dead is unearthed. that is us. the world will tell us how the world will end. but remember this the next time you ask us if we know how to swim.

cotton

sweat through the garments made to let us breathe
but just a little.

sweat through the discomfort made to make us
uncomfortable
but just a little.

harvest in august bittersweet tea, deep south temperatures
from sunrise to sunset
but we miss the summer months just a little.

burlap sacks graced our backs bent over just a little.
destined for greatness we wiped the sweat from our brows
just a little
and sung church hymns under our breath and thanked the
Lord just a little.

our feet touched earth so we knew God was still within us.

we sat with spirits because we showed resistance in life and
in death.
we know death isn't the death of us.

we were bruised fruit squeezed until three hundred pounds
of white gold was put upon

our backs making the land fertile.

until we were beaten and made brittle.

we knew it would never be enough.

soil

who made you soil?

who made you believe you were our life support system?
who allowed you to cover the bodies you buried?
the families you detached. the kings and queens you
removed from their land.

who made you soil?

you removed the teeth.
broke the bones.
you cut the tongue.
calloused the hands.
you scarred the feet.

raped the innocent.
burned the flesh.
whipped the thoracic.
left lesions on the lumbar.
brutalized the body.
allowed the screams to be your tranquility.

who made you soil?

pattern paths of plight through Plymouth

Abraham Pearse Blackamore, Black pilgrims

the nutrients in which they clasp are the mixture of the tears they captured, the blood they drained, and the sweat they squeezed. them. you. us. the decomposed organic matter you claim is nothing more than my ancestors you owned, sifted dry, spread throughout the land you stole. you scattered melanin in your fields because despite your hate you understood the value of Black gold.

wet.

you dampened the fertilizer to improve your growth.
you discarded the remaining carcasses and grinded the bones into ash in order to get high on what you could never be.

who made you soil?

each day starts with a dry mouth, numb, unable to taste anything but the bitterness of bitterness. i've dragged this body around, silenced with cotton underneath my fingernails, the smell of chlorine in my clothing and soot in my thick nappy dreaded locks from the lies you burn.

when the texture is dry, unable to absorb new beginnings, it is depleted and no longer holds its moisture.

when the texture is firm to the touch, sandy, silky, chalky and clay-like from the mixture of the blood of the Black bodies it can no longer detain.

the texture and structure of the soil will lose its influence on the behavior and what it was used for and need to be replaced.

who made you soil?

seed money

no salutations,
prior to restraint.

startup capital kidnapped still wearing their African garb.

blood money,
doused in unpaid debt with demands and sacrifices

beyond the chewing of the cotton root.

they search for the bodies,
in unmarked graves with an overhead not as costly

as a noose over their heads.

rigid reproduction reveals resistance,
digesting calomel and turpentine, accidental smothering,

and the case of Margaret Garner.

it is a labor of love,
lucid that unfixed themselves,
to keep their loves out of labor,
protecting their production from the horrors of bondage,

and all they endured.

neither,
the prevention of a maroon, redemption, or emancipation
can't stop caring for their own bodies,
defying the devil's applause,
denying their sinister greed.

the first time

because i have not existed to let my scars be the misguided history of whips, chains, pale knuckles to the Black scabbed palms of the lineage of the Black scabbed palms of the Black scabbed palms of abuse. because i have not existed to carry wilted and inherited practices of punishment. i will choose violence for my peace. i will choose violence for my mama's peace. i will choose violence for my grandma's peace. the first time i attempted to fight my father i did so with the protection of peace and love in the pursuit of peace and love. sweaty palms. loose half curled fists with no intention of being thrown by my sides. a scowl pulling the skin on my face in tightly. an older reflection scowling back at me. too scared to ask for a hug but in desperate need. intimidated but boiling deep inside like a pot of grits on a southern stove. i wanted to shed this blanket of rage with the warm embrace only a Black father could offer to give his Black son. but there we stood. muted and harmed by the unjustified harm of the unjustified circumstances of the unjustified repression. the first time i attempted to fight my father i walked away with a cocktail of emotions and questions wondering if i should've thrown a punch or stayed out of grown folks' business. i attempted to fight my father on two other separate occasions without a punch ever being thrown. each time losing pieces of myself to protect pieces of my mother that may never be returned. maybe the pieces of her lay scattered somewhere unknown next to the pieces of me next to the pieces of him. maybe this is what they mean by a broken home. he went through years of internal conflict and dysfunction attempting to comprehend why when he acted in love it looked like pain until his pain needed him to act in love. with remorse he confessed to the dark pathways he traveled at the expense of his family to soothe the debt of his trauma.

the first time my father attempted to hug me…i hugged him back. i was twenty nine. he died eight years later, not before returning the pieces of me i thought i'd never get back.

freedom comes with release

freedom comes with release
but the noose dangles wickedly
let go anyway
experiences become a part of us
entangled in our identities.

teenage Black boys with limps and stutters

today in school i learned that my grandparents' grandparents' grandparents belong to some white folks. i'm confused. when they say "belong to" do they mean family? if so, i belong to my mama and daddy and nem'. apparently, they worked for them. apparently, they fed them good. apparently, they gave them somewhere to sleep. apparently, my last name is not my last name. it belong to them white folks who my grandparents' grandparents' grandparents belong to. i didn't learn that last part in school. my mama's daddy taught me that. apparently, they let us borrow the name or was it keep the name? i don't remember but apparently, my grandparents' grandparents' grandparents fought in the war, or was it wars? my mama's mama said us Black folks still fighting a war. i don't know what she means by that. they said having Black folks fight in the war helped bring down some of the costs. they said the white folks were arguing over how much the Black folks could help with the farming, the cooking, the building, and the repairs. i don't know but i thought we were all family since the Black folks "belong to" the white folks. shouldn't family help family? they said the Black folks could be free like the free white folks if they help kill some other white folks but if it's free why does it cost so much? did you know that my grandparents' grandparents' grandparents help build the white house? that's an odd name for a house built by Black folks. i didn't learn that in school. my mama taught me that. did you know my grandparents' grandparents' grandparents built many of the universities? ironically, i didn't learn that in school either. my daddy taught me that. they say i don't read too well. apparently, my grandparents' grandparents' grandparents weren't allowed to read at all. apparently, that's all they gon' teach us about the "involuntary relocation." apparently tomorrow we gon' learn more about how some white folks separated from some other white folks so America could be great but i feel like they teach us that every year.

how do you wear your Black skin?

i feel fancy.
i wear my skin as a flowy garment.

free. i repeat. free.

flowing, free, and full length.
freedom within this body.
within this Black skin.
comfortable.
tailored.
the best of both worlds.

transitional Black skin producing more melanin in the sun, redistributing its beauty into a lovely darker shade.

but they come for it.

notice where in me it hurts.
and when it hurts.
and why it hurts.

mundane acts of life changed by the imprints of past and current defects brought on by the fraying of american society.

if you wanted to purchase a slave, take your nigger to the physician.
if you wanted to save your nigger
health equals wealth, take your nigger to the physician.

our skin, Black gold.
our labor, Black diamonds.

untrimmed threads: hanged.
broken stitches: broken limbs.
puckering: battered.
needle damage: whipped.
faulty patterns: discarded.

vibrant colored textiles.
bold designs.
abstractly embroidered robes.
beautiful prints.

how do you wear your Black skin?

i hope
proudly.

...never born as slaves

we were never born as slaves...

...don't mind these calloused hands tender, strong, scarred, used to plant, tend, and harvest cotton, sugar, rice, and tobacco.

...don't mind these bruised feet with heel spurs, cuts, puncture wounds used to bare the weight of these burdens.

...don't mind the flogged back or the dislocated shoulder, shackled feet, and a series of chronic illnesses.

the missing tongue that was cut out of my mouth to hide my voice but they failed to remove the microphone.

...don't mind the noose that dangles from trees with roots soaked in blood.

we plant seeds when under duress so the torture is just a blessing of the land.

those are not whips, chains, stacks of broken Black bodies.

we were never born as slaves.
we are not unfree.

we do not toil away.
we are not mute.

our Black bodies are not possessions
and our minds are not confined.

…don't mind the tears, the gloom, the pain.

…don't mind the burns, the cuts, the scars.

…don't mind these leg cuffs and enclosed spaces with dirt floors.

we were never for purchase.
we never stood on auction blocks.
we were never captured by the slave patrol.

we sing.
we dance.
we drum.

we are mathematicians.
we are doctors.
we are architects.
we are engineers.

we are parents.
we are children of God.
we are community.

we were never born as slaves…
we were born as kings and queens,
and that's who we remain.

reparations

fuck you.
pay us.

for the culture.

II

gaps

in the downtown section of Jersey City where no fewer than a half dozen housing projects stood, almost no part of the neighborhood escapes their intimidating prosperity-squelching presence. fire hydrant summer swimming pools. late friday night manhunts. broken jump shots, ankle breaker crossover dribbles, and basketball games of twenty-one on cracked pavements of asphalt squabbles. imperfect surface prone to breakdown over time. left behind were the poorest, most disorganized non-working families; societal casualties. inner city Black community medieval fortress. fully loaded clips. windows boarded up. chunks of plaster crumble from the walls and a collection of soft toys and flowers signifies the spot where young men were recently killed. these were just boys. block beaters with heaters and drug paraphernalia. snatched chains, cliques, gangs, with gold memorabilia. subsidized residence turned into crack dens. no cure for the ills of the severely distressed. heavily concentrated. deteriorated neighborhoods just beyond the city's thriving central business district. the drab high rises confront hundreds of loop-bound commuters each day. fumbling, funneling, trafficking drugs ignoring the suit and tie government elect while blaming the blue-collar suspect. their crime graffiti, garbage, urine-stained stairwells, and broken elevators testify to years of social neglect. and mock the dreams that built them. ikea furniture in project living rooms. jumpman logos, hilfiger polo baggy jeans, tan timb boots.

crack vials, weed smoke, heroin balloons. fatherless children of women grew up and went astray. many blighted projects became a lawless place. unsafe urban decay with gunfire a nightly occurrence and murder commonplace. but we were told this was our home and we listened so we stayed. it was a place of the rankest degradation with a lack of government funding, support, and participation. we live in fear. young men freely use drugs in the common areas. where thirty-eight-year-old mothers wheel around twenty-two-year-old sons left crippled by drug-related shootings where bullets went astray. where work and marriage were abstractions, distractions. where we still yearned for the love of an absent father. blessed nonetheless due to the formation of sunday morning faith factions. bird on a wire. like a drunk in a midnight hour we have tried to be free. the human spirit's struggle against inherent frailties and external pressures often result in futility. bedeviled. by hyper-segregation, urban decline, and de-industrialization. these weren't good times. scratchin' and survivin'. poverty in color. no huxtable in sight. this was florida evans family real life plight. we told stories and dreams of kings while standing next to fiends dribbling a basketball hoping to one day be seen. bird box. blindfolded poverty paradox. we remain unseen.
i was just a Black boy born and already plotted against.
whether you call it assisted living, a project, a tenement; either way it was a fucking experiment.

and the gaps between rich and poor,
white and Black,
privilege and punishment.

they still exist.

where i'm from

i'm from parallel parking, stolen car radios, and quarter waters on hot summer days. i'm from bodega papis, doritos between buttered rolls, and paper bag chip parties. i'm from paper bag forty-ounce swigs, bus stop corners, everybody's uncle hustling newport loosie cigs. i'm from contact smoke highs, milkcrate dunk contests, and uncertain, its depression lows. i'm from where pretty boys wore low-cut fades, braids were worn by those who were gritty, and b-boys wore high-top fades. i'm from holiday cookouts, friday night manhunts, hidden knives, and thugs who spit blades. cash stashed in socks, gallon milk plastic tops with washers, and tar added to play tops. i'm from jumped fences, fiend mothers, and kids playing tag daily using those skills to evade cops. i'm from double dutch, no respect for open necks, slap boxing, yo mama jokes about mothers who treated us like their own children. i'm from leftover family sunday dinners, church clothes laid out early sunday morning, late-night crab shacks, and burger spots on corner blocks. bulletproof glass liquor stores, barbershop dialogues, street sermons and bootleg mixtape cds on every other block. i'm from where swimmers never swam, and where sprinkler systems never made big enough puddles to teach us to hold our breath. i'm from where large bodies of water were for beach days, mini vacations away from the cluster. i'm from clutter and mischief-encased cement structures in poverty. i'm from where they called it a project but they had no intentions of finishing it one day. i'm from where absent dads had absent dads who had absent dads where dads went to prisons due to fabricated wars and sons grew up to become absent dads and they blame an entire culture for absent dads when all we talked about as Black adolescents was missing our absent dads. i'm from where nightmares happen during the day but we still daydream. i'm from piss-stained hallways, crack houses, abandoned buildings, and apartments heated by ovens in the winter. i'm from families piled on top of pallets on linoleum floors blocking doorways. i'm from where your uncles treat you like little brothers and you don't call your friends friends but instead they are your cousins. i'm from where trauma exists, conflicts, regrets, and repents. i'm from generations of college graduate hopefuls to first-generation graduates.

i'm from praying for better days.

i'm from where love resides.

monday morning in the projects

and therefore weekend days are marked by their sense of fluidity. and out past the shadows on the other side of the tracks in a space and time where they put distance between the proclaimed vulgarity, leaving us isolated claiming us untamed, unkind, violently. the depiction of an invisible world's uncertainty. solemn and gloom if anything is lost. we attempt to plant seeds and in deteriorating moments, we cherish. we grip tightly in what subtle beauty in which the eye beholds from the fire escape vantage points of simply being grateful. we know blood will be spilled, we hear the loud noises at night but this narrative has been authored to encourage the planting of plight. we extend life by becoming strangers to the dark, the night and summers are when we experience the removal of the most light. unexpected images within the brick structure we shield our innocent from those sworn to protect. staggering within sin, remembering moments, repeating bible terms, we somehow absorb the possibilities, and what has been learned, while continuously casting off the many ways in which they attempt to take our lives.

them

this is the prelude to a bruise. scars revisited. the prologue to the wounds and the aftermath of lesions. this is the midst of a seismic shift. this is a state of grace. this is the dismantling of the white album, "what have The Beatles learned from negroes" fate. this is the complex cultural four elements from the South Bronx to Staten Island. this is the re-gifting of the purple tape. this is how we fight for our lives and how we see what is included and what is at stake. we are more than the many that try to end us. we are more than the brick and mortar of the concrete prisons you try to enslave us in. we are more than the faces painted black, caricatured, tambourine rattled bones gaudy swallowed-tailed coats and striped trousers. we are more than the jokes. we are more than the subliminal stereotypical sensationalized ideals ingrained into coded language bigoted. we are more than the deeply seated pathology that we are predisposed to be talented athletes for the sheer joy of your entertainment. we are more than the up jump the boogie pop and lock electric slide of the soul train lines. we are more than emulations, depictions, omissions, and your obsession with the casual "slip of the tongue" admissions. systematically subhuman censoring racism politely. we are more than your underpinned usage of the n-word conceived blurred lines. we are more than your terms of endearment and your "us versus them" concealment. impurities refined. where rebranding equals trendy. hard-pressed. i can't breathe too lightly. what will become of us? the present sells silence through blood-drenched asphalt. ripple and riddled with chalk outlines of Black bodies brutalized by barneys. fickle and fiddled with blocked outcomes of Black bodies neutralized by political parties. our past is history paved over, gone through, gentrified, dismissed, and glorified. unacknowledged. deemed not important enough to remember. unidentified. what we face. finding bright spots in promising potential. unbound, touching everything until unburied. rebirthed ancestors' flesh and blood until reparations are provided for their flesh and blood. unconventional blemished ballad muddy water blues. four hundred years of oppressive exit wounds and out of the sun comes Black boy joy healed hues.

nothing but grief

nothing but grief
despite death being written into the contract of existence
we mourn
lost is the endeared and boundless consciousness that no longer exists
we prayed for food, shelter, and safety
we prayed for moments like this
we are tethered to regrets
feeling abandoned
losing a loved one;
to finally understand the moment someone dies;
is not when the love ceases to exist
we bury the living
like we have the power to reverse an hourglass
while keeping our distance
six feet apart
until we are six feet apart from the soil to the pavement
a unique sequence disperses our soul from its shell
freeing it from containment
slanting rays and the warm orange tinge in the sky
the upturn of the corners of the mouth
the crinkle in the eyes
but a frown is swept under a rug
drug, misunderstood, left and ignored
departed

we find our heaven
earth offered us an abundance
but it's not the same
love offered us a symphony of hues
the sluggish summer air violet blues
but somehow we only remember the rain
after years of remorse, grieving, and sinning
we settle our debt with what we couldn't live up to
and embrace what we became
but why must we die wilted?
why must we die fragile?
why must we die with our eyes open, breathing, and alone?
don't put flowers on the grave
if you failed to provide water and sunlight to the garden
don't mourn the roots
if you chose not to appreciate the blossom.

e.n.d. grief

(for Grandma)

the significance of everything dulled, misshaped, discolored, broken, and buried
the thickness of the Middlesboro, Kentucky mud resembling the thickness of blood
funeral flowers seem to live longer than the bodies they lay quietly to celebrate
to mourn your flesh and blood is to cover the powerless moon by harnessing the wind of what has been and what will never be again
the sweetness stored in the petals dried by the sunlight
death by the rays that once provided life
she was skin and bones, her bones delicate, the wind crisp, her skin no longer tar
her grip no longer vice-like
her hair short metallic shade
her eyes cloudy velvet cake sweet but seem to fade
seeming faint and slow still swift and sharp
cracked lips still curved, tongue still, her hand sits still in my nervous palm
yet you'd still fancy her glow
sweltering in worry we are children of the slums
we will face endless toil if mother earth can no longer speak
dry bones turn to ash stored

and into the heavens so bright
the wounds crackle the sound of fire ablaze
when it is final hours we pray for peace, months have passed
she slipped in peace
her bible markings in margins resembled her prayers
whispered
hands clasped on bended knee
she slipped in peace whisked away in peace
seeds planted the roots strong believers only die when they
trust death when they bury their deceased
tree branches will grow to give the most leaves the most
light
greens, oranges, yellows, reds
leaves will fall
mourn not
it's beauty not grief
the significance of everything dulled, misshaped, discolored,
broken, and buried
hollow hills, brown terrain, the scars, the lesions, the flaws,
the hope, the faith, the love
she lived so she could find God and within God she found
her peace

flowers in the snow

(for Curtis)

it hurts. the heaviness of it all. but we existed knowing that flowers didn't bloom in a mixture of broken stone or gravel. and if violins can be both beautiful and cold, we could be both beautiful and cold. a preteen attempting to find the perfect balance of adolescent angst and artful chaos while protecting my innocence. intelligence. in those disordered days, you detached the clutter.

carefully omitting curse words from reciting rap lyrics residing in two different worlds. the pronoun "we" becomes "they" far from us extending the reach of the vacuum of separation. struggle comes with fear and the anchor balances dangerously close to the tipping point. and calm looks too much like stillness. and stillness looks too much like letting go. in desperation, we hold on. maybe for too long or maybe not long enough. who are we to judge?

we were poor but mostly noble and mostly kind. but i still find myself thinking about the heaviness of it all. i still find myself thinking about you. death turns the best of us selfish. wishing a loved one remains ignoring the days they drown in. death doesn't always occur when our last breath has been taken. sometimes we suffocate in life. sometimes the body is deprived of the love it needs to survive. sometimes that love is taken away when they become breathless. sometimes the oxygen is the last to go.

dear uncle.

hidden beneath the layers of sharp conflict, incurable sorrow, absolute silence, buried underneath the ashes in the midst of the thick stale warming smoke, lies the man who became my father figure; my protector, who accepted his wounds to shield those he loved but now you must rest.

it's okay to rest.

the winter years are often the coldest but there can still be beauty when the flowers are placed in the snow.

he was never heavy.
he's my uncle.

his love is weightless.

won't you come celebrate with me

(for Aunt Linda)

and into the heavens
comes equal parts fire and earth
carrying love as water carries nutrients
lessoning the burden like the air we breathe

the sun struggled to rise in her passing
mourning the morning when her shine dimmed
cracked pavements we walked transformed into valleys
elongated depressions in the earth's surface
stalked by casted shadows
we listened to the dark
because we were raised to capture the night
anytime we suffered a loss

her passing in the winter's freeze
forced the spring's thaw
compelled the deeply shaded gloom against its will
until the summers bloom into september's fall
brought bitterness to sweetened air in which we breathe
made forever seem like too long
life seem too sour
made us clench our teeth
we miss her but we inhale attempting to still breathe

without her

though we shall be starved for her embrace
we don't suffer the same loss as the moon each time the sun rises
repeating church hymns, harmonies
clutching the thick church organ moans
grasping every hallelujah
amen
while we worship the Lord
because in her rest we shall celebrate

as she would not accept in life or death that we be undone
unraveled
or in contempt
or in contrast to our convictions
as we continue to put our trust in the Lord
even when we can't conquer the complexities of illness
we counter the containment
and the conclusion of our physical form
as our stream of consciousness continues

she taught us that

now won't you come celebrate with me
won't you come celebrate with me

she is here
she will always be here

do you see that flowers bloom?

do you hear the buzzing of the plump honey bees?
do you smell the warm citrus scent?
do you hear the shuffling of a deck of cards?

she is here

won't you come celebrate with me

i have a stubborn memory
it refuses to let her go
i won't ever

let her go

every day is a funeral

every day is a funeral
as a child
on the bad nights
i would grip my tear-soaked pillows tightly
mumbling some resemblance of a prayer incoherently i have
yet to learn
praying the screaming would stop until sleep became my
escape
i could smell the booze on my dad
his pores became intoxicating swimming pools his drug
addiction would proudly become
immersed in
my mother would battle my father's demons
but i would get hit by the debris
i watched an uncle join the military
another find comfort in his sickness
and the others be let down by the american dream
i watched my family self destruct from the inside out
we argued over financial instability
we ducked, dived, and hid from gunshots
we tight-roped to avoid eviction
we stood on our tippy toes just to see over the poverty line
and we lost our balance to addiction
this is the position we were in
this is what i had to witness

as a child
i misunderstood this conflict
so i would shout to anyone that would listen
"i'm going to save us"
followed by
"when i get older, i'm going to go to college"
but our environment kept killing us
our addiction kept killing us
the government kept killing us
we keep killing us
your. america. keeps. killing. us.
and you want to know why i'm so pissed off about education
because i needed it; to save my family
but instead
every day is a funeral

call to Pop

yesterday i called my father to wish him a happy birthday but he didn't recognize my voice. my larynx trembled, producing the sound that uttered my next carefully selected words through my now dry mouth. i said, it's me, Pop, it's your son. Pop was the nickname i gave to him when i was just a little Black boy searching for my father figure, as he, my biological was trying to figure out how to be a father figure. but i could never bring myself to call him dad. there was an awkward silence, a deep breath, flashbacks to unforgiving memories and disappointing moments. i felt pain. i felt grief. my mom named me Carl after you; it can't be that hard to remember. i write these poems to heal. why did i even call? why do i even bother? i held back tears, remained patient, hoping the voice on the other end of the phone would finally give me value as his son. after a brief pause, he hesitated before he spoke and said, who? i didn't know if i should blame his elevated age, the loss of grey matter due to his over three decades of crack usage, or was it simply because we haven't spoken in a while or was he still upset at the time i made the decision to finally stand up to him. not yet a man but not a boy no longer willing to accept the pain in my mother's eyes, in that moment i wasn't willing to back down. it hurt to repeat myself but i did. i said, it's me Pop, it's your son. at this point he recognized who i was. i took advantage of this moment; i said, happy birthday Pop, i would like to see you today if i can. he said, maybe later. i have to go hustle because that's what hustlers do and there is $30 waiting for me and he chuckled and said, you know how your father is.

i said that i do. i said, before you go there are some questions i need to ask you. i said, i wish you would've helped me transition from a young Black boy to a man. i said, i wish i had someone i could call dad instead of a nickname. i said, despite your lack of effort you raised a scholar who grew up in the trenches around thugs. i said, my friends grew up having three careers in mind: pro athlete, rapper, or becoming the first drug dealer to never get caught. but i avoided stereotypes as much as you avoided family dinners. i said, did you even have expectations for me besides not going to jail? i said, why didn't you introduce me to the Lord? i said, why did my mother have to argue, kick, and scream to get you to provide money for school clothes. i said why did i have to turn on the TV to find a male role model. i said why the numbers 7-23-81 never held any significance for you. i said, how come you never remembered my birthday but i remember yours. i said, why didn't you attempt to protect me in a world that has tried to label me as a nigger since birth? i needed your protection, where were you? i said, why when i entered therapy in my late twenties the only topics that made me shed tears were the ones about you. i said thank you. i said thank you because of you i never sold drugs. i never used crack. i didn't hang out in the streets, and in any relationships i was ever in i knew how to come home at night.

i became a first-generation graduate in spite of you. and one day my son will call me dad instead of a nickname. because if he ever needed to find me, all he would have to do is look right next to him. i remember when my grandfather died. i watched as my mother's bones ache, her tear ducts became a desert, and each day she prayed to have her dad back as she tried to find the strength to continue on. that taught me to remove you from the coffin i placed you in inside of my heart. Pop, do you remember when you use to make us grits and eggs for breakfast, lunch and dinner because that was literally the only thing you knew how to cook? Pop, do you remember when we watched super bowl twenty five together when the giants beat the bills when scott norwood missed a field goal to lose the game for buffalo? and you said buffalo was your favorite team so they became my favorite team as well. Pop, do you remember that time you hugged me and whispered in my ear that you were proud of me and said that you loved me?

i wish i would've had the courage to ask my father all of these questions but instead, i said,

Pop, after you get that $30, give me a call.

i would like to take you out to eat for your birthday.

ashes

my father's ashes arrived in the mail today.
thirteen pounds of already brittle bones turned to dust and
burned flesh.
absent flesh.
just as i remembered as a child.
i wrote
"not at this address"
"return to sender."
i needed a dad
before i needed an angel.
i hope God,
God
gives him his wings.

III

mother is the name of God

two hundred and seventy-three moons, peace be still, eternal sunshine reflection of brown hues, exiting the earth's womb, peace be still, mother is the name of God. a love supreme. side stepping imitations, avoid limitations, fabrications, the devil's work facade, seeds planted in the sweetest of wet fertile soil to birth a king. purposeful pause, rejoice and sing, the gift is the person who births us. a mother's love rooted in the existence of her purpose, rise up to the fundamental story of Black faith, that sows deep within the sun, a reflection, a mirror, her face, a mirror, a reflection of him, a mirror, he sees the reflection of God, in her, raising a wildflower in the cratered concrete surface of poverty, with a history of violent collisions, involuntarily beautiful visions, perhaps ever-present deep-seated color of love, dreams, fantasies, ideas with aspirations, over forty-three hundred alternate religions in search of prosperity, she, we are within her, our mother, our wonderwall, frail bodies and images of broken women crying over their slain sons, slain bodies, the healing is the necessity of it all, old wounds fractured into forbidden paths leading to a bastard's trail, earthly eyes strain to peek through the winter's cold, the wilderness will, hearts hardening, but her tenderness will prevail, brown skin, confront critical conversations to love within, our mother, our earth, our God, where the color of love begins.

the fear of a Black mother

(for Pattie)

the stoop.
the porch.
the distance between the chipped discolored concrete steps
and the end of the curb.
my playground.

the distance from my mother's bedroom and my ability to
hear her call my name. the sound.
my body clock sunset.
the vibrations attuned with the street light.
she wanted me to miss the sunset in order to see another
sunrise.
her fear.

she birthed a bundle of joy when God.
answered her prayers.
'till.
my Black body turned my future into a
question.
a boy.

i was just a boy.

but her unattended grief was assigned to her
by a country that viewed Black death.
like spare change.
discarded.
low value.
what is left once you break down something with purpose.
pieces of worth clustered together that
can no longer be whole.

tears.

i have never seen my mother cry.

her mother sleepwalking in her pain
taught my mother to do the same.
her grief.
a cloak.
disconnected leaning on stoic expressions.
wondering what age did i turn from
"so cute"
to
"so scary."
her fear.

my mother read bedtime stories each night
that begin with
"don't wear a hoodie"
"don't make sudden movements"
"put your hands up and keep them up"
"don't go into white neighborhoods alone"
because the happy ending only happens

when you make it back home.

her fear.

at night
she gave each hug like it was for the last time.
holding on tightly
daring anyone who came to harm me
to attempt to leave without taking her too.

her worry.

she tucked me in at night with "i love you"
hoping my comfort was enough protection.
she crawled into bed with a prayer
slept with her eyes open
her ears golden.

she could hear the thunder before the storm.
the danger before the plot.
the pain before the hurt.
the sickness before the symptoms.

she could never rest.

a shared heartbeat.
a labor of love.
the security of the womb.
my birth created an exit wound.
the emptiness
of bringing something fragile into a cruel world

knowing she could only do so much to protect her son.

she taught me.

she taught me
how to reattach my joy to my smile
my love to my warmth
to put breath back into my lungs.

she taught me.

Black is not a reason to be ashamed.
a reason to fear.
a reason to walk in silence with my chin touching my chest.

keep my head up.

my eyes open.
my heart open.
my knowledge plentiful.
my fist clenched.

she taught me.

they believe i'm a threat.

because i am.

while she may live in fear for her son.
once a Black boy.
now a Black man.

to never treat my Black body as a burden.
to never treat my Black body like i'm an intruder trying to escape my own skin.
to never treat my Black body like a death sentence.

she spent nine months perfecting the pigment of my melanin.
and she would be damned if they brought her son's life to an end.

so don't worry.

treat your existence as a gift.
be present.

and breathe.

when they call you a thug

when they call you a thug.
it is because the word nigger tastes sour on their tongues.
unsweetened.

swirling each letter around in their mouth
until it forms in the shape of degradation of others.
slowly sticking the tip of their tongue
on the backside of the top row of their teeth.

thug.

spit out with ferocity.
spit with the intention of harm.
spit out bitter, savor the sweet.

you called me a nigger with your eye contact
long before you savored the sweet.

your body language defensive.

your movements and gestures show that you're insecure.
unapproachable.
closed off.
hostile.
disinterested.

you spit racism verbatim.
perfectly pronouncing every syllable before you dare to move your feet.
the hate you give resides where you live.
birthed beautiful babies.
watched them grow
and then taught racism to your kids.

when they call you a thug.

just know it's intended with the same sincerity
that gave permission to your ancestors to sleep in the house.

they say it with fear.

blinded by the proclaimed power they fear the assumed powerless.
turned a racial slur into an adjective.
they touch their hooded masks like Braille.
feeling every stitch, every fiber of their ancestors.
the ones who claimed land, people, pillaged the poor and rested on outcomes that stated we were brutes but i question who were the real savages.

when they call you a thug.

they do it with disdain.
giving power to a word leading to dissension and confusion.
they want to tuck you in with divisiveness
have you sleep with paranoia and awake with pain.
to be hated for being birthed to the skin you proudly claim.

carefully navigating misconceptions
embracing the African pyramids and royalty in which we came
is to be the sun and be hated for your shine after the rain.

when they call you a thug

and allow the syllable to pour out of their mouths and drip onto the ground
leaving an outline of hate in the form of a stain.

it says more about them than it will ever say about you.

bus stop. Black man

and the Black boy cries for his mother.

when you're a young Black male living in the hood they teach you how to throw a punch on the same day they teach you how to use your voice, pray, and to define what Blackness means to you.

these are survival skills.

on the same day, i learned about the birds carefully laying eggs and bees pollinating flowers, i learned how they seed, sprout and plant drugs to harm Black bodies in Black neighborhoods and end life cycles.

on the same day, i learned that the porch offered enough protection to calm my mother's nerves and the streetlights were a warning of the violence that may occur, i learned what gunshots sound like when they ricochet into your first-floor apartment wall.

on the same day, i learned about sexualities and the importance of acceptance and love, i overheard two men arguing calling each other racial slurs.

i never did learn how to properly throw a punch.

i never learned that violence can come from those you least expect.

one day i learned the anagram for secure is rescue and those who are meant to protect could be the ones you need saving from the most.

shift ended. leave work.
bus stop. bus late.

police cars. bus late.
Black man. bus stop.

police cars. Black man.
bus stop. bus late.

bus arrives. Black man.
go home. Black man.

get home. Black man.
be safe. Black man.

police arrive. bus stop.
get off. Black man.

scared stiff. Black man.
handcuffs. Black man.

illegal search. Black man.
police knee. Black man.

police brutality. Black man.
police brutality. Black man.

go home. Black man.
mistaken identity. Black man.

get home. Black man.
mistaken identity. Black man.

be safe. Black man.
mistaken identity. Black man.

go home. Black man.
trauma. Black man.

get home. Black man.
trauma. Black man.

be safe. Black man.
trauma. Black man.

trauma. Black man.
trauma. Black man.

trauma. trauma.
trauma. trauma.

go home. Black man.
get home. Black man.

be safe.
Black man.

and the Black man cries for his mother.

i was twenty.

write about freedom

the young man was shot forty-one times while reaching for
his wallet
the thirteen-year-old was shot dead in mid-afternoon when
police mistook his toy gun for a pistol
the unarmed young man, shot by police fifty times, died on
the morning of his wedding day
the seventeen-year old unarmed Florida teen was shot and
killed by a neighborhood watch volunteer

i said i wasn't going to write about freedom any more
because i can never get back what i lost in the fire
songs of survival
songs of freedom
repetitive rhythm

children wade in the water find passages to freedom
i said i wasn't going to write about freedom any more
looming dangers of disobedience or perceived infractions

whipped
shackled
hanged
beat
burned
mutilated

branded
imprisoned
raped
i can never get back what i lost in the fire

Blackened; charred remains
the faintest glow of embers
Black dust hung in the air
pale morning light like a skeleton watched us hang
memories of warmth
in those ashes lie our photographs

still moments
inferno; Black smoke billowed into the heated air sending a
distinctive aroma
i can never get back what i lost in the fire
all of my heroes wore crimson suits filled with torsos of
bullet wounds with deferred dreams
i said i wasn't going to write about freedom any more

you fit the description
step out of the car
hands behind your head
neck tightly gripped restrained from breath
chokehold
handcuffed
beat
tazed
shot
administrative leave
repeat

license and registration
put your hands where i can see them
body camera malfunctioned
he did not comply
he's armed with Black skin
a hairbrush
and a pick with a Black fist

Black males in america
you're Sisyphus
punishment without the trickery
the weight of five institutions
unfair conditions, propositions
and white police officers who shoot before asking questions

there are more of us walking the corridors of a prison than
the halls of an educational institution
overcrowded prison with not enough scholarships

a witch hunt they can't admit
fifty years of the war on drugs
there are too many of us still to convict
how do we forget
we forgot about burning cities as cities still burned

remember what they proclaimed to your ancestors
they were considered a fraction of a man
one part slave
one part prisoner
one part nigger

and two parts gun pointed with a hair trigger
you're doa, sol, and fucked
out of the birth canal

your freedom isn't free
they police our bodies like they can copy and paste to
replicate our dna
your freedom isn't free
your roots are covered in Kunta Kinte blood
your Black thought enslaved
with no quest to love
undone
as things fall apart
loose stitches
there is wisdom in these lyrics

Black man
listen to me…

your freedom isn't free

the burden

the burden of male Blackness manifests itself differently
disproportionately, more often in a coffin, fatally

"i'm not insignificant, repeat it back"

that is what she said to me

"they may treat you as a target"
"but you're not a criminal, or a suspect"
"your life will be lived beautifully"
"you're beautiful"
"Black boy, you're beautiful'
"don't ever think differently"

but she was cautious when she spoke
fear in my eyes

"you're a Black son, my son"

a tear dropped from her right eye
she continued but hesitated

"reach for the stars"
"but be prepared to have to reach for the sky"
"know your rights"

"know when to fight"
"your complexion shouldn't be a lesson"
"but be aware of the streets, the police and the devil's affection"
"walk in faith"
"live your greatness"
"never adjust your crown"
"and be the light"
"son, be the light"
"rather yet be the sun"
"let the universe consume you"

"be the sun"

cut dead

left to my own devices i disappear.
far too many minds closed for the truth.
justice failed Trayvon Martin the night he was killed.
a verdict setting his killer free.
Black boys are denied the right to be young.
dangerous.
interchangeable.
guilty until proven innocent.
sophisticated thugs.
expendable.
they are not invincible.
closed mindsets.
invisible.
divisible from fearless dialogues.
one nation, indivisible, ridiculed with liberty and justice for some.
i am invisible.
i was never more hated than when i tried to be honest; to tell the truth.
truth is living when living is a lie.
living is truth/living is life.
living is love/living is life.
what are you living for?
i'm living for life.
i'm living for truth.

the truth is the light.
cut dead.

the american body carries the virus.
racism. bigotry. one-sidedness is synonymous.
the residual racial cough is contagious
so what's the fuss
because
it's killing only us
spread. dead. The american body.
spread through the american body
the plague.
meanwhile, Black boys are killing each other wantonly,
deliberately
it is sometimes advantageous to go unheard
to be unseen,
rewired brain chemicals changing mental circuitry
shifting right and left brain symmetry,
chemistry
they say we die by the gun in poverty
ignoring that internally we are suffering mentally
financially, struggling with ptsd, depression and anxiety
cut dead

because we kill those who are not the same
Black, gay, become slain
forced to choose between sexual identity, race
invisibility
or end up dead
pray and support the LGBTQ+ community
our silence allows others to fill the vacuum critically

to lead the debate in our absence
potentially
this is tragic
hashtag
Black girl magic
Black girls matter
pushed out
over-policed
and unprotected
cut dead.
this bullshit can't be accepted

forced to mask their insecurities and pain
taunted for their nappy roots
it's a paradox
interplay of privilege and vulnerability leading to oppression
marginalized; pay attention to the clues
they feel ugly on the outside
never doubting their inner beauty
beautiful cocoa brown skin
thick braided locks
gorgeous brown eyes
america
i count on my sisters
despite your "pretty for a Black girl" lies
each night before bed
i count my sisters
because of the bounty you put on their lives
quiet strength
see them
hear, affirm and love on them

because the human race makes us all kin
despite our differences
we all face adverse childhood experiences
hustle hard
but we are still the only face that face a.c.e. in the hood
misunderstood

Black boys and girls are denied the right to be young.
dangerous
interchangeable
guilty until proven innocent
sophisticated thugs
expendable,
we are not invincible
closed mindsets
invisible
divisible from fearless dialogues
one nation, indivisible, ridiculed, with liberty and justice for some
we need to change the rules
dominant white cultures and ideologies
don't let them extinguish you
let the fire burn within
support Black pride
that is commendable
we are not invisible

cut dead.

will they ever accept us?

will they ever accept us?
is it a relief or a nightmare; being a citizen in america
duck, dodging, despair of stereotypes declining symbolism
avoiding stereotypical american materialism
growing contempt for electoral democracy
and political-cultural liberalism
vacate, vent or pursue politics as a professional
but they've had a political patent
stronghold since colonialism
mocking with fervor
social hierarchy
and the rule of the elites
fictitious felicity
and the void of fervent patriotism
so hold on to your Black culture
raise a fist in the face of the bluest of eyes
your darker skin has always been a sin
look at the hate in their eyes
they playing for keeps
reinvent and revise
why they despise,
reboot, and reprise supremacy; ironically
unresolved terror
looks for pity amongst the struggle of their fallacy
follow your dreams,

all the rules,
avoiding schemes,
things are not always as they seem
don't look for mercy or leniency
the shade of your skin is a tad too dark
for clemency
respecting your neighbors can get you killed
music too loud
asleep at home
too many niggers in a crowd
jogging
or even less
bitter, sardonic, probing
they'll never respect us
or even less

accept us

IV

write about love

have you ever set out to write about love but ended up
writing about war?
romance looks like cannons.
a bouquet of flowers grenade.
pin pulled blossom.
two lips kiss.
like a carefully planted mine.
their bodies touch.
war.
his arms extend around her neck.
a pointed rifle.
each bruise.
a battle lost.
each excuse to cover his abuse.
shrapnel.
she's a prisoner of war.
her body.
a city ravaged.
her body.
turns to dust.
he sets out to conquer new land.
have you ever set out to write about love
but ended up writing about war?

broken flowers

from the earliest days of life we end our evenings on our
knees. start our mornings with grace. peace be beside us as
we journey through fate. steady the pace. smile for a change.
disheartened by the broken flowers still attempting to find
the beauty in detached petals, as the once blossom shrivels
and fades.

i know my mom was once in love with my dad.
i know my dad is still in love with my mom.

i know this hurts right now but maybe broken flowers heal.
maybe their roots buried deep resisting the forces of wind
and running water or mud flow
or bruises or cuts or harm to the flesh is to feed the
development of food and beauty
to nourish and not erode
to stimulate and support once fertile soil now depleted
or maybe broken flowers dried by the drought of the
summer's heat restore the joy in its soil
recapturing its need to reproduce love which initiated its
blossom to begin with

but first they must stop holding onto the bitterness of the
vivid stigma and styles or threads of grudges fancied wrong.

stop yelling,

because your child can hear.
stop breaking things,
shards of glass will one day cut the bottom of a willowy barefoot as a
reminder creating a new sense of pain.
stop smelling of cheap booze and other women,
silent gloom doesn't fill voids with anything but unripe bodies
stop abusing because your words are sharp
creating cuts that turn into wounds that heal into scars
stop crying,
your tears become your child's tears, your fears become his fears.
stop having the police come to the house,
bars are barriers between buried burdens and bottomless remorse
stop hurting each other for the sake of hurting each other,
in the distance, awakened and scared, you're hurting another

because the petals loosen with the vibrations of animosity,

all flowers experience cold periods, long frigid nights of winters shivering stems, and become dormant, blocked, unprotected.

if a petal is cut off a flower, that petal can never grow back.

something once beautiful can become limp, lifeless, distorted, and black.

something once beautiful can become…

me.

story of Jahseh

the headline reads:
Black male accused of domestic violence
found dead.
missing is the context of a young man with a story that is
complex and deeply rooted in the textures of his childhood.

this man.
a painted picture with layers upon layers of contrast
provided by each stroke creating a multi-layered effect of his
past.
Jahseh.
born into the warm loving track filled arms of his teenage
mother.

his birth certificate was the void of his father's signature.
premature.
three pounds, four ounces.
just a pound more than the dope his father was in prison for.

age four.
the first time his mother's best friend fondled him.
robbing him of his innocence.
while planting the seeds of a victim turned offender.

age five.

the shape of a palm
a bruise in the form of his mother's right hand on his right arm.
still calm.
a bruise on his inner right thigh.

a welt on his back.
a punishment he did not ask for but his smile surprisingly remained intact.
age six.
the first time Jahseh tried to stab one of his mother's boyfriends.

the sixth boyfriend in six days with the absence of a last name and a first name of john.
the blush on his mother's cheeks matched the bruise left around her left eye.
she was a working girl.
age eight.

Jahseh no longer knew the appropriate way to cry.
instead, his lacrimals produced sand that ran down his cheeks like an hourglass.
his tear ducts now a desert.
a place where thirsty emotions go to die.

nine
Jahseh turned nine on nine eleven watching the towers crumble felt like a metaphor to how he felt on the inside.
his parents crashed into his hopes and dreams one at a time each piece of debris left in the wreckage

another disappointment
buried was his potential
ten

Jahseh called another Black boy a faggot because he looked
at him weird.
not understanding the kingdom this young man possessed
as the Black boy joy ran through both of their veins
eleven
Jahseh found a stack of letters hidden in his mother's dresser
under a dress addressed to him

they all end with the same question
why don't you come visit me anymore?
p.s. i love you, signed dad
twelve.

not the first time Jahseh hit a girl
but her no met the backside of his right hand
he pillaged her body like columbus discovering a new land
he treated her consent like a promise that needed to be
broken
the stem plucked from her cherry

thirteen.
fourteen.
fifteen.
the juvenile detention center became Jahseh's vacation
retreat.

it was as if his travel agent wore blue with a shield

he would imagine the cage as a beach house
he found peace
in here
he didn't have to watch his mother suffer

in here
he didn't have to feel the fingertips of his mother's best
friend slowly destroy what never was
in here
he imagined the comfort his father must've felt being in
prison
but not having the prison in him
sixteen
seventeen

eighteen
Jahseh woke up with a white powdered substance around his
right nostril,
a warm gun in his right hand with a bullet wound that only
pierced flesh
but not deep enough to compare to the wound left by his
flesh

and blood when he was born that is still fresh and warm
he didn't deserve this
nineteen
twenty

Jahseh attended his mother's funeral
he couldn't bring himself to sit so he stood
in the back dressed in all black,

and like all Black men are told they are supposed to do
he stood strong trying not to crumble
stumble
but if you looked close enough you could see the cracks
twenty one
the headline reads:
Black male accused of domestic violence
found dead.

the void

to linger and lurk in what you believe to be whole, to be nestled in a crack den you never accepted the invitation for, to be subjected to an extended stay to the function of dysfunction, to hide behind cracked yellow stained teeth, scattered bruising, dirt resting under your fingernails, and hand-me-down, worn and tattered name brand clothing two sizes too big, or two years too small, to follow the footprints of bare feet of those taken too soon and to endure in spaces that have copyrighted your second-hand future for a worn path to failure and to be born to encounter a breach of peace and desist acts of sabotage only to find in order to discover a life of peace you must first come to blows.

it's exhausting.

and there is a void.

Ronnie

the aged Black boy cries…
but i've been here before
an aged Black boy carrying around his parents' wounds
seamlessly since the womb until the stitches come undone
the first repeated night i thought
in the dark the bleeding hearts grow in the shade
does that make me beautiful?
the mouth moves without speech while the tongue is at rest
inviting the devil to slow dance, i think we don't
put dead things in comfort
nor do we tame trauma responses in a cage

my teeth have long been rotten
yellow-stained, my hair
slowly fell out leaving patches
sweeping what was left
into drifts, until i gave in, shaved, exposed the
perimeter of my scalp, the circumference of my
heart brittle, my family tree roots filled
with rock salt, fallen foliage, now everyone just leaves,
the damage has been done, i appear naked and unafraid

young boys shouldn't have mothers who mourn
their adolescence with their mother's tears
have you seen my mother?

her whereabouts still escape me
cold stovetops with stomachs in conflict with self-hate
you'd place luggage of shame into my palms and a
thumbtack trail along my barefoot path
vulnerable but i have already become numb and i cannot feel
by the time i reached age thirteen, my uncle jonesing claimed
to have the remedy, i haven't been able to get this monkey
off
my back since, nor can i remove these devils from
atop my shoulders,
have you seen my mother?

every day the day dies, you can't get back tomorrow
as we experience more death in life than we acknowledge
and society forgot what my innocence remembers
i was handsome once, i even smiled
and thoughts about the end of the world
looked like just another monday,
i have been left behind more times than
i have stolen, and robbed of my dignity more
times than i have robbed, and i have consumed more
drugs than i have sold, can you blame my addiction
to euphoria when it is boundless
attempting to break the bondage since my birth
internal imprisonment shown and never seen
boundaries with borders keeping family at a distance
attempting to remove entanglements

i felt the end of me before i knew the words, still waiting
for my permission to live before catching hell,
death quietly cuts in on my courtship, the devil

tap dances, heel and toe taps but i remain motionless
you cannot always take away the diagnosis
but at least you can treat the symptoms

or at least stop staring…
or at least tell me where my mother is.

e.n.d. love

i've been stuck in this monotony of worshipping with the bible closed; full of faith; transparent wondering if God still loves me as life unfolds; my mouth open suicidal; hard of hearing; no sense of taste; touching the moisture in the dampened earth; blinded by the sunlight every time she sunsets life gets cold; or the times when my father reappeared; only to disappear to reappear; it was always dark; it was always cold; but he still managed to cast a shadow; left me to believe there was still a sense of light; emphasis upon his death was foreshadowed by his absence in life; Genesis; the first book in the bible; created by the God above; birth; and how every nigga deserves love; tears never made the flowers bloom; years never made the grief be removed; prayers never made my grandmother's life resume; if hugs equal love why am i always the only nigga left in the room? left to consume; the emptiness that comes with isolation; contemplating and processing why i was the reason she left so soon; taxing to heal; surrounded by plants and condensation; trying to reverse my own evaporation; love bombed; confession; i'm a couple of years from having a couple of fears come to fruition; attraction; i'm supposed to know how to form a couple and provide affection; when i have never seen a couple form love without the eventual subtraction; insecure; seeking love from another; anxious-preoccupied attachment; separated from a mother's hug; distance distraction; times a lack of discussion equals disruption; still wondering what i'm in search of; stuck between compassion and the end of love. every nigga deserves love.

V

i wish i was dead

a gunshot in a quiet place
impotent and fanciful daydreaming
still breathing
a slow mental rewind through the past
mundane emotional collapse

God, why am i still here?

i don't remember the exact day that i stopped loving life
and started chasing the most curious
invisible wound
but on that day
i became a shell casing of myself
looking for an escape
from where disturbed memories existed

i didn't want to die
and neither did the bodies of
the frail countless community castaways
who choreographed their deaths with connected conviction
after clasping onto the calloused pieces of themselves that
remained cold
barely breathing

people vanish in this world

remain unseen
search for the truth in order to heal
only to discover
shards of glass in the place of puzzle pieces
rendering their inability to feel

prayers turn into suicide notes
asking God for forgiveness
but hoping to not see another day
i was blessed with life
but plagued by the inverted concave
of happiness where joy used to realm
my days are shallow and bare
abrupt
slight
and
extraordinarily dreary
to only see the light when the sun shines
is to be removed from the beauty of the sunset.

ever since

i was born at the center of emergency and been in crisis ever since, foreshadowed the stench of burnt ashes ever since, planted, pained, persisted, scattered and returned to the earth's wet soil ever since, i grew from seeds enriched with love dispersed into divots cratered by the dried cracks of the heels of captives ever since, a new born caressed by his mother's glare, cradled by his father's stare, cut by their distress ever since, newly born, a child of the ghetto, the grandson of milk, honey, and wisdom, rolling stones and confusion, the streets have been watching ever since, scraped knees, scratched elbows, bruised shins, and crooked teeth ever since, tight wool curls, bowed knees, fearful ornate eyes, and been hurting ever since, bound bowls, boundless bids, lost boys, and channel zero ever since, gospel hymns, strange fruit, strapless boots, and reoccurring sins ever since, breakbeats, drum loops, nineties fashion, and grimy lyrics ever since, fatherless fathers, suspicious sirens, provoked paths to prisons, and voiceless victims ever since, i have been seeing the world through a lens of the pain of others, i have been ruminating, remembering, and removing silence from these lips ever since, i have been Langston Hughes ever since, keeper of the ashes, being vulnerable and finding a safe space to repent, i have been searching for forgiveness ever since, i have been asking for forgiveness ever since, ever since,

i have been trying to find my way to heaven,

to God
to mercy
to a pain-free existence

ever since

ever since

i have been born, i have been in crisis ever since.

pour heavy

if we must die let it be with a bouquet at our fingertips. remove the obstruction and focus on relishing in the time we spent. the irony in our deathbed not being a place for carcasses. its catharsis. understanding without rain no flowers; life is heaven sent. pour heavy. pour heavy until the overflow threatens to drown the sorrow of yesterday and yesterday becomes the hope for today. calendars should return hearts and flowers not abused innocence in anguish. just as tears leave trails, days can be left unfulfilled, we tend to filter blessings and kickstand pain, take the spotlight off of joy and claim clouds of sadness as we sit in the rain. we forget to build openings for emotional tectonic plates not allowing acute ache to escape following the voices of elders and possibly meeting their ugly fate, unlived, we can't bargain with time for forgiveness, or wait to mend broken fences with relatives after sickness. some words are better left said, spoken, and revealed; some poems are better lived.

pretend

i looked for death in God, wanted to die for my sins, researched the means to the end, living a lie in a life of make believe, i could no longer contend with an identity playing pretend, the devil living rent free paying for my father's end, is what i was convinced was the devil's fee – ever since i was ten, watching my father's friend further my trauma with addiction…in the kitchen cooking cocaine, was this trauma the devil's finder's fee? tail end of industry versus inferiority, social anxiety in the recess of my mind, adolescence missing, i had to pretend my father's lies didn't bother me; time flies i failed in every romantic relationship, is it time to admit those lies now apply to me? praying for forgiveness, trying to pretend that i didn't wish for a different childhood to begin again, splinters in attempts to mend broken fences, mistakes take place despite intentions, offering an apology, accepting consequences when acceptance doesn't come in the form of an acceptance of an apology, avoided every pitfall in my life, they said everything would be all right, you'll never be like your father, i believed them, that was before i knew of the trauma that grew inside of me, they lied to me, left empty, still attempting, pretending what i grew up trying to be, competing with the kid that envisioned a better me, a version looking for closure trapped inside of my father's plea, accepting God's vision, wondering what He envisioned, wondering if he still sees forever inside of me.

left shimmering

things are not always as they seem. from time to time tears are reluctant to stream down still clear and unblemished cheeks. nineteen different sweet curves of full lips with six resting in sorrow. it is easy to mistake a smile for joy and ignore the gloom. decent and silent. a smile can be a stoic grin and bear it expression. bottomless and dampened by the rigidity that is life. the rigor reformation removes the rekindling of rosiness turning a bloom to a burning sensation of life expectancy. we lived because we were birthed. we died because we are charred. given wax wings and told we could reach the sun. "i care about us" can be heard only to hit the ground and discover the truth. we weren't born to go to the light. we were born fluorescent.

but left shimmering.

instead of absorption, we became a reflection of you.

a transmission of waves passing through a medium of withering woe of worry.

a cycle of cold leaving us shivering.

radiant heat from the sun interacts with the earth allowing life to flourish; until artificial light cracks and discolors the surface;

leaving us behind with nothing but the fallen sun and the cold shivering darkness of night.

what Black boys pray about in the dark

grandma's cornbread both bitter and sweet. birthday cards with dead presidents gently placed on the inside. the first winter's snow. God's protection over my mother. i pray my father stop cutting rugs with demons on irreversible dance floors. uncle Charles's parole. Uncle Floyd's sobriety. praying that Uncle Curtis finds his way. praying Uncle Williams's sermon works this time.

we pray for love that reminds us of the warmth of a sunday family dinner. we pray for the bruises to heal, sometimes our own, sometimes another's. we pray that the news of your best friend's cousin junie being killed was just a rumor. we pray that math test gets canceled and we pray for the final scores of basketball games. we pray for growth. we pray for rain. we pray that one day we don't have to boil our water, sleep three to a bed, or have our parents support a family of four on minimum wage. we pray for government assistance but not food stamps. we pray for the policies that incarcerate our fathers to change. we never prayed to leave the hood. we prayed that the government would stop putting drugs there. guns there. stop putting dead Black bodies there. stop putting cops who harass, torment, and kill there. we pray they put those boots they speak so highly of there. we pray they put jobs there. proper funding there. love there. we don't pray when we break the law but we pray the law doesn't break us.

i pray these fists no longer have to be trophies that sit on mantles.
i pray for forgiveness.
i pray for change.

i pray my poems are not a living will. i pray my anthology doesn't become this really long suicide note that i started writing at birth.

i pray when i get to heaven my ancestors are there. i want to hear the truth about how they lived and how their breath was taken away.

what do Black boys pray about in the dark?

we pray to see tomorrow.

to do the things, to feel the feelings

which created a nasty abrasion that started to bleed. a poet retreats into somber and at six-years-old for the first time a Black boy has learned to tuck his pain into shadows that will follow him throughout his light. remains stoic in the face of vulnerability. he will wear tough love like a badge and go through life devoid of reciprocity. applying pressure externally to wounds that only heal internally. his voice box muted, tongue swollen, the words discreet, the strength of a thousand ancestors but we hope to one day acknowledge ourselves.

Black boys cry in solitude.

have we been raised as Black sons to feel unprotected in the glares of white america? sentenced to life in a body we never learned to trust. or feel. or to present to a society that believes the term ghetto is a setback to settle but we sift and soar. we thrift and pour until our pores sift and soar.

but why can't we feel anything?

as Black boys we are handed the first brick and as Black men we build barriers between intolerance and feelings. toxic masculinity versus sanity to provide and protect our family. we gather lesions in our leisure because it can hurt to simply exist.

which created a nasty abrasion that started to bleed.

Black best friend
Black nephew
Black cousin
Black grandfather
Black uncle
Black brother
Black father
Black son

let those Black boys cry.

sugar in our wounds

sugar dissolves more rapidly in hot water. sugar has healing properties reducing bacteria turning bitter to sweet. sour to sweet. your puckered dry mouth relaxed, damaged gums, salty taste shattering taste buds, you can't let us be so you rub salt into wounds into skin you broke because of skin you broke because of skin you broke. tomorrow we shall exit as flesh and blood and bones and skin and limbs and joints and hips and wrists. we come out but we tremble so violently as we exit the sweetness of the proliferation phase of our wounds. the healing laceration mixes well. there is sugar in the medicine. they say we can be a man as long as we are not Black. they say we can be Black as long as we are not gay. maybe that's the crime society has tied to our person integrating two marginalized identities in which either one is not fully accepted. Black is not an offense. Queer is not an indictment. Black is gorgeous. Queer is ferocious. our person is not flawed and our existence is not a burden. we are tired of leaving behind, from what is left behind because we had to detach what was left behind for your comfort and our safety. for your peace we've had to hold on to our pain for so long so don't ask us why we still grit our teeth. from pulpits to schools to parks to nightclubs your overt messaging is clear and you come in mass for our peace. but the remodeling phase is complete, we reattached and we have been willingly evicted from our wounds so today we shall exit as flesh and blood and bones and skin and limbs and joints and hips and wrists. we come out whole as you attempt to create chronic wounds but ever since Marsha we prefer our person to be hot and sweetened anyway. leaving salty taste to those who prefer bitter because bitterness is sharp. bitterness is pungent. bitterness is disagreeable. bitterness is fear. bitterness is anger. we look to resolve and heal in the ways sugar heals and dissolves sweet even if it touches flesh.

VI

Black becoming

we didn't sit around thinking about how to do wrong until doing right worked against us.

somehow Black health feels intentional.
somehow Black health feels like rebellion.
somehow Black health feels like power.

the creator has given me the sunrise and the sunset so i can see the beauty in the stars and the sun peeking through the clouds.

i can see the beauty in the rise and the fall.
 i can see the beauty in the affection of the warmth and the distance of the cold.

maybe, sometimes we feel too much.
maybe, sometimes we don't feel enough.
maybe, sometimes we feel too deeply.

an abundance.

maybe, sometimes we don't deserve to feel at all.
maybe, sometimes we have good intentions but we make bad decisions.
maybe, sometimes love just isn't meant for everyone.

maybe, sometimes we should just run away

but often nobody will come looking for us.

maybe, sometimes the blackened barefoot soles of our feet are a reminder we've done enough running.

maybe we should stay and embrace it all.

this is where i leave you

last night i stayed up late attempting to write the ending of my story. i foreshadowed this conclusion since chapter fourteen when the rising action developed slowly into the climax and now i just crave the resolution. i don't blame the crack that occupied my dad's veins. he was attempting to find his light but instead found euphoria through poison that provided temporary peace to the indefinite pain. i don't blame the fire in my aunt's apartment that nearly burned to the ground when i was just a boy. the flames were a warning to the pain that would smolder in my lifetime. i wish God would've sent smoke instead. i don't blame the contemplations. i never felt irrational holding an open bottle of pills. i never felt ashamed perfecting a hangman's knot in a noose. i never felt a future cutting slits in my wrist. without these scars, i would've never found the gift of the present. my past chapters would've had pages with bent corners because i seem to always save the place in my life where it hurts the most. i learned to be patient as the sun absorbed into my melanin. i sat still listening to the raindrops hit my window sill. i confronted fear and look down when i stood on the edge of the cliff. because depression is like falling to your impending death. at first, you want to be saved as fear takes over your body but then you find calmness in the breeze. until the time comes when you get tired of falling and impatiently waiting to hit the ground. your body shattered upon impact. finally resembling the carcass you've been dragging through the streets every single day. feeling like the entire world is pretending you don't exist. all this time i've been trying to put out fires with gasoline teardrops. i've been trying to swim with no limbs. i've been trying to make peace with something i cannot see. something i cannot touch. something i cannot speak. but rather something i can feel. something i can hear. something i can breathe. and to those who have loved me, i'm sorry because you could've never known that i was flammable. to my ex-girlfriends, i'm sorry for hurting you. you had no idea that loving me would've been like trying to hold on to a grenade. at some point, you have to decide whether to let go or to become a casualty. i was hot to the touch, sour to the taste and our courtship became the sweetness lingering on the tip of your lips that only became bitter once swallowed. once remembered. to my mother: you raised a Black king to never back down from anyone or anything. i'm cut, bruised, and battered. look at my wounds. i promise i will never stop fighting. to my Black brothers, internalizing only makes depression eager, salivating at your unconscious assimilation i challenge your whisper, silence doesn't win this fight, this is passed down from generation to generation, this is not a battle. this is a war. this is not a symptom. this is a disease. you cannot run. you cannot hide. you must stand face to face removing the slave mentality. you must be willing to ask for help. take your Black male pride and your masculinity and allow yourself to be open

speak.
be humble.
speak.
be vulnerable.

speak.

and to depression i no longer need you to sign a permission slip to allow me to be happy, to feel loved, to feel blessed, to feel free. you were never supposed to be a part of my existence but yet you sat down in my faith, took long walks inside of my heart, and took up residence in my mind. you attempted to burn me to the ground from the inside out like you put drugs in my dad's veins. like you attempted to burn down my aunt's apartment.

but i'm still here
i'm still breathing

because the search for everything starts with the search for self and now that i finally know who i am and who i was born to become

depression i say to you

this

is where i leave you.

i am that i am

i find myself trying to talk less but say more
blazing a trail to a Black future
i am that i am
take my sandals off approaching the burning bush
they knew too well the stench of burning flesh
swarthy, dusky, reddish-brown soil
synthetic fabrics
brown protective melanin skinned
essential oils
internalized feelings of self-worth
the intersection of imagination
leading to a future of liberation
Black earth
glance upon the brightest visible stars
maps with constellations of ideas
ancestors deprived
a travesty
birth a new reality for young majesties to live
facing our history and ourselves
experiencing the embodiment of resistance; resilience
floating tombs in dead oceans
on the high seas
the smell of death
the sounds of screams
blessedness of answered prayers

Black women
ubuntu
i am, because you are
Black queens
Black royalty
reclamation of the throne
seeking His wonders, forgiveness
love in the form of a sign
it was written; Nasir jones
unrehearsed versus of parables
Mansa Musa
live from the underground
a king remembered in time

the dialectic of double consciousness

whereas the dialectic of double consciousness in the souls of Black folk hinders our ability to measure oneself due to the constraints of those who oppress, we confide, curate and confess code switching as a means to no end to provoke our best. a line drawn in the sand. we search for our placement on maps full of negro paper towns. redlining to keep us contained. sacred burial grounds. Black genocide. tree ornaments. moving target. the back of the bus. tyrant, we didn't forget. whereas you believe your oppression is a thing of the past, we carry around master degrees to own our master to a degree. we still carry around slave names. while you carry around false claims. merchandised and monetized pledge allegiance to the flag drenched in our blood. take a knee. ball a fist. protest your right to resist. whereas John Lewis walked the bridge in Selma. in defense of a better tomorrow. Black face. the minstrel show. jim crow. home shouldn't be where the hatred is and all struggle isn't packaged the same. i have walked the cracked pavements in the hood. stood where drug dealers have stood. i have watched my brothers be victimized and put in a cage. quieted my rage. i have been racially profiled by the police, professors, and while making minimum wage. worked in corporate cubicles. and did what i had to do to walk across the graduation stage. i have lighter skin but they still consider me less than. do the math. one light skin mother plus one light skin father equals a lighter child. but they question my melanin. but this Black skin is my kin. it doesn't automatically make me a chameleon. ask the police every time they get near. they try to catch me riding dirty but to live in america makes this shit seem fair. i live in oklahoma. where a man was lynched yesterday. bear witness to the racist murders taking place in this nation. his lifeless Black and brave body hung motionless. Donye Jones fought for a better america but this is america. whereas, according to amendments, policies, guidelines, and bylaws i come from a long line of niggers. and i'm still a nigga. and i'm still a slave. still images of Emmit Till in the grave. and i'm still Black. and i'm still brave.

healed Black boys

a room full of Black boys, Black men have gone quiet, again.
the silence is too familiar as Black bodies sit in graves far
more than they sit in church naves.

we have lost another Black body.

who is it this time?

we already lost Virgil, Nipsey, Omar from The Wire,
George, and Chadwick.
my father, Uncle William, Grandpa William Sr., Uncle
Boobie, Uncle Curtis, cousin Chris.

we are running out of space to engrave their names in places
we can mourn them in peace.
we try to respect the deceased but their privacy is a
shattering kind of silence.
we have already sent the collection plate of grief around for
the second time in hopes of acquiring whatever tears remain.

we are exhausted.

to know Blackness is to know death so we sleep in
catastrophe.

i asked my mother do Black boys heal or do they succumb to accumulated trauma?
she referred me to God, and when i asked God He said to turn off alarms and seek the truth.
He said to embrace His unconditional love and seek acceptance because that's when i'd find relief.

healed Black boys do cry.

at night i think about when this Black body will turn into ashes.
and i pray my remains are turned into diamonds that sit on the earth's mantle.

so i can continue to shine.

if i could come back i'd come back as a Black man, again. Black men given their wings as a compensation for how their Black bodies were put into ruins.

i'd come back as Donny Hathaway because his voice felt like freedom and i'd heal his shattered bones. i'd come back as Langston Hughes because he delicately dismantled cliches giving the Black working class a stage to exist. i'd come back as James Baldwin, now a misunderstood ghost would return to uphold the value of those racially and sexually oppressed.

as they carry out more Black bodies the silence is deafening. and imprinted under our skin.
but we will heal.
our ancestors traveled across dead oceans

and sacrificed life not to lose lineage despite the brick wall.

we are beyond the experiment.
we are beyond the disease.
we are beyond the abuse.
we are beyond the incarceration.
we are beyond the racism.
we are beyond the brutality.

we are beyond the murder.

we refuse to relinquish our Black bodies so bury our dead in African soil and watch us rejoice in the rebirth of our kings and queens.

because we are beyond the wounds.

to the members of the establishment

to the members of the educational institution and establishment: how can a person understand? give due recognition to the Blackness of a Black man or woman unless that person reveals a fair amount of information about him or herself. i am asking listeners to accept the truth of what it means to be white in a society created for white people. i am asking listeners to tarry with the ways in which they perpetuate a racist society. the ways in which they are racist. i am asking listeners to not turn a blind eye or a deaf ear to the prolonged cruel or unjust treatment of people of color. i am not asking you to nod politely, bristle, change the subject, launch into a disconnected political rant or stand in stunned silence. i am asking listeners to listen intently with conviction and have the willingness to invoke change. the truth can't be told; it has to be realized. be willing to listen to an opposing point of view. privilege isn't about what you've gone through. it's about what you haven't had to go through. Malcolm X once said, what does a white man call a Black man with a Ph.D.? a nigger with a Ph.D. James Baldwin said, love takes off the masks that we fear we cannot live without and know we cannot live within. let me express the vulnerability that i wish to receive in return. we don't talk much about the urgency of love these days. the type of love that risks not being reciprocated and refuses to flee in the face of danger. the type of love that demands that you look at parts of yourself that might cause pain and terror.

the type of love that demands that you find comfort resting in your discomfort. there are times when you must quiet your own voice to hear from or about those who suffer in ways that you don't. you must be willing to accept that your privilege creates, provokes and prolongs our oppression. there are times when you reap the benefits from your comfort in white spaces as we suffer for being Black and people of color. but your comfort is linked to our pain and suffering. i sat in classrooms in white spaces on campuses built on the backs of my ancestors. while you sat in boardrooms in white spaces full of white faces changing facts pandering to investors labeled a bunch of criminals. walking the path of school to prison pipeline isn't a subliminal. ignoring is ignorance and perhaps makes you ambivalent to the conflict and pro-containment as you rest in your contentment. but rest is for the weary. i speak these words because King no longer can. because Chuck D told me to fight the power and Nas told me the world is mine. i speak these words by any means necessary because my vocal cords are a revolution and we are determining the future at this very moment as we teach you that breakbeats with rhymes can defeat hidden agendas and stale policies frozen in time. these words are a gift to you. bear in mind. some gifts can be too heavy to bear but i give these words to you freely, openly and respectfully. you have the right to refuse or accept without any obligation to those who are being oppressed. but please understand this;

the convenience of your silence does not go unnoticed.

e.n.d. life

i'm burning. strangled by smoke i felt my skin burn. in this space, i breathe carefully. lungs still inflamed. fine particles of smoke coat and layers harboring the air in which i breathe. my body is triggered. dead things pull hair triggers for weapons i didn't know my body possessed. my body has felt the ghost that anticipates my gentle movements. i never met the Black boy that owned this body before the fire. he might be ashamed of how i used this body to stand in harm's way knowing the damage it would sustain. scraped knees, broken limbs, flat bruises, sex used as a tourniquet to stop the flow of pain from what now resembles a cadaver. at night sometimes i mourn this body. sometimes i mourn Torino's body. the fire put us at a distance but we remain inseparable. i have spent a lifetime trying to process things i don't remember and feeling things my body won't let me forget. i have long attended the memorial for this body but each day i am alive the viewing leaves me awake. i've discovered love in this life but childless out of fear that trauma frightens my genes, ready to turn my offspring's body into a haunted house. my dad lived his future in the past escaping the devil's grip but surrendering to fate. i wear my father's name as if it was heated with fire and pressed against my skin. i wear his scars because he couldn't carry them all. his burns are my burns. when his life ended i inherited them all.

groundwork

i still question why i have never been afraid to live or die but to feel.

or
why trauma makes me feel uncounted amongst the counted.

or
why inducing pain frees victims who were once victims?

or
why did my grandmother tell stories as if my life depended on it?

she took a wrecking ball to her experiences
hoping the rubble left behind would be uninhabitable
and deter her kin from residing.

yet the streets were still littered with the undead
so we joined the damaged and became infected.

unaware,
the memory was the medicine
and the healing will always begin with the stories we tell.

speaking the unspeakable

accurately cites the heaviness of the collapse
allowing you to be heard.
allowing you to heal.

grandma was right.

to reconstruct
you must remove
and then restore.

the rubble was the dismantling.

her stories

laid the groundwork.

deconstruct

what if you were called a different color?

the texture of your hair, size of your nostrils, your build, your intellect, and whether or not you are safe to be around is called into question.

what if you were...

deconstructed? stripped from the skin that brought you equal parts shelter, armor, and harm.

skin and bones spliced together like the tattered and frayed ends of a noose with a touch of love, handled harshly, tart, with a hint of vindictiveness.

unfinished. centered/grounded. different shapes and sharp edges, disguised/bold.

pieces configured dna reflect a troubled history, making peace while still worshipping and trusting in the Lord while on a path of the unknown. where some say your life is meant to be forgotten, so they forget.

but what if Blackness was a symbol of gravity, instead of spoils to rotting repotted land, an invisible force pulled us toward one another?

what if we needed time to relax, dance, and sing?

what if we put love as a centerpiece on a table surrounded by hate? could we exist in a place of refuge?

what if when they deconstructed and pulled us apart, we shed the skin like damaged layers of disease from exposure to environmental elements of irritating particles and gracefully walked away from what they hoped we would succumb?

we remain keenly aware of the murmurs, the rumblings, but Blackness will not simply and slowly fret away under the pounding of the threat of a storm, the wind, the rain.

we prefer to look at it as lessons in light.

the shadows are too afraid to make it a dwelling and the good still resides in fountains of purity even when salted a tad to remove bacteria, redeeming our skin's natural glow.

we don't fall apart.

we rebuild.

they didn't stop then

we won't stop now young Black boy/aged Black man
precious Black girl/tired Black woman
your story is being told

it has been extraordinarily quiet

i know you hide your pain well/as do I/too well

and deaf ears have created distance/silence has created
shame

but before midnight and the moon sings
a lullaby to the setting sun
you must find the courage to speak your relief

dig your heels into the African acidic soils/dark orange
stagnant/waters

frail surface/hardened

we have escaped/drowned
we have been liberated/incarcerated
we have marched/beaten
we have preached/shot

cried

sung

laughed

fled

died

the color-line blurred the crack epidemic claimed a community
education disparity driven by prejudices
institutionalized racism
modern day genocide

unleashed dogs/fire hose cannons/nightstick bludgeons/false accusation whistling

WE HAVE SURVIVED IT ALL

we have existed as
kings
queens
slaves
captives
targets
martyrs
activist
abolitionist
free thinkers

freedom writers
presidents

Rodney King video footage

Amadou Diallo bullets

Jesse Washington lynching

George Floyd suffocating

Sandra Bland hanging

WE HAVE EXISTED THROUGH IT ALL

not without strain
not without worry
not without hardship
not without grief

but we have always had each other.

don't forget, and out came the sun again

and today you've been weeping again.
and this morning you remembered that all the dead Black boys look like you.
and it is the fourth anniversary of your father's passing.
you try not to think about the burning but the smoke has never cleared.
Black boy to Black man, you're not the unraveling of the world around you.
you're not the half-taught anguish and despair in which you come from.

you didn't set that fire
you didn't lift that bottle
you didn't pull that drag
you didn't snort that crack
you didn't pull that trigger

you have worn a mask to cover up your scars not knowing that the way you have healed imperfectly is beautiful.

you have turned countless tragedies into triumphs.

you are loved.

Black man, you are loved.

you are loved.